thank you

FOR ALL YOU DO

Made in the USA
Las Vegas, NV
01 May 2022

48270656R00072